GOLF JOURNAL

Copyright 2015

All Rights reserved. No part of this book may be reproduced or used in any way or form or by any means whether electronic or mechanical, this means that you cannot record or photocopy any material ideas or tips that are provided in this book.

DATE: 27/7/15

Commonly done: pull, top and push slice times normally done 20 times.

Uncommonly done: push and shanked times done before on normal basis 10 times.

Rarely done: flicked and over swing normally done 3 or 4 times probibly.

DATE: _____

DATE: _____

DATE: _____

DATE: ───────────

DATE: _____

DATE:

DATE: _____

DATE: _____

DATE: _____

DATE: _____

DATE: _____

DATE: ───────────────

DATE: ───────────

DATE: _____

DATE: _____

DATE: _____

DATE: ———————

DATE: _____

DATE: _____

DATE: _____

DATE: ———————

DATE:

DATE:

DATE: _____

DATE:

DATE: _____

DATE: _____

DATE: _____

DATE: _____

DATE: ─────────────

DATE: ───────────

DATE: ───────────

DATE: _____

DATE: ───────────

DATE:

DATE: _____

DATE: ―――――――――

DATE: _____

DATE: _____

DATE: _____

DATE: ———————

DATE: ───────────

DATE: _____

DATE: _____

DATE: ───────────

DATE: _____

DATE: _____

Printed in Great Britain
by Amazon.co.uk, Ltd.,
Marston Gate.